From the Hood to Hollywood

A Guide to Investing for Millennials

Chukwuemeka Nwaopara

For information about special discounts for bulk purchase please contact Chukwuemeka Nwaopara at: MajesticCyberEnterprises@gmail.com

www.MajesticCyberEnterprises.com

Printed in the United States of America
ISBN: 978-1-7353543-0-9
ISBN: 978-1-7353543-1-6

Book Design: SuccessWriteNow.com
Consultant: T. Marie Bell (www.tmariebell.com)

FROM THE HOOD TO HOLLYWOOD

DEDICATION

I dedicate this book to my grandmother, Cecilia Obiesie. Your fearless spirit and serial entrepreneurship helped mold me into the man that I am today. You were a true matriarch and raised eight children to be intelligent, courageous, and self-sufficient. You instilled the significance of entrepreneurship into each of us. Thank you for your love, support, and wisdom. I love you.

TABLE OF CONTENTS

1. FINANCIAL LITERACY

Financial literacy is the key to success! Some people fail to realize how much their thinking affects their decisions. To be a Boss, you have to think like a Boss. This is an important concept. You must never sell yourself short. Believe it or not, your thoughts guide your mindset. It's actually more important than the knowledge that you have. Your thoughts are constantly shifting and evolving. So think wisely.

"Money without financial literacy is money soon gone".

Financial literacy is the only way to empower our generation to use their mind and ideas to create wealth. Before we can have generational wealth, we must first change the way that we spend money. We must change our mindset regarding how we value money as well. It's imperative that we use our knowledge to solve problems and create innovative ways to produce money from our minds. A person who works for money will work forever. But, a person who has money working for them can retire at will.

"It's not what you make, it's what you can keep."

Many celebrities and athletes struggle financially after their prime due to the lack of financial literacy. This could have easily been avoided with the proper mindset. That's why it's necessary to change your mindset to make money work for you. You must understand how money works and invest your money wisely so that your kids' kids can benefit from your financial decisions.

After you learn how money works, you can then build systems, solutions, and businesses to help service your community. You can create legacies and businesses that will feed and hire your family and community.

It's critical to change your mindset and control your spending. You should never spend money at an establishment that will not hire you. You should never spend money at an establishment that doesn't respect you as a customer. You should never spend money at an establishment if the owner will not spend money at your establishment. Once this basic principle is learned and practiced through the power of financial literacy, we will be able to maintain more money in our communities. This influx of financials will help us better partner with one other on major business deals to sustain our community and become more self-sufficient. Self-sufficiency is the goal. When we are totally self-sufficient we will not depend on any government agency or corporation for food, water, housing or electricity.

2. CONSUMER VS. PRODUCER MINDSET

Consumer Mindset = Rico

Rico loves to shop at fancy stores that would never hire him or his peers. Rico owns a brand-new luxury sports car from a company that would never hire him either. He loves to stay fashionable, so he purchased expensive watches and jewelry from a well-known jeweler. However, none of the establishments where Rico shops on a daily basis would ever hire him. As a matter of fact, he is closely followed and heavily monitored whenever he enters these stores. Yet, Rico still continues to spend his hard-earned money with these companies in spite of the ill treatment that he receives as a customer.

Rico is a well-paid professional who works at a large corporate company and earns a salary of $110,000 a year.

After taxes Rico earns approximately $7,500 a month.

Rico's Monthly Bills:

Rent-	$1750.00
Car Note -	$750.00
Car insurance -	$400.00
Jewelry -	$1,500.00
Utilities-	$250.00
Trips (Hotels/Flights)-	$2,000.00
Restaurants-	$850.00
Total:	$7500.00

After receiving $7500 a month in income, Rico spends his entire salary. He is left with $0. This is the true definition of a consumer mindset.

Producer Mindset= Theo

Theo is a well-paid professional that works at a large corporate company and earns a salary of $70,000 a year. After taxes, Theo earns approximately $3,850 a month.

Theo's Monthly Income:

Investment property-	+350.00
Stock Portfolio-	+150.00
Car listed on website-	+250.00
Online sales-	+450.00
Real estate consultant-	+450.00
Total:	+$1650.00

After receiving $3,850 a month, Theo also earns $1,650 a month from his investments and side hustles. Theo is the true definition of a producer.

Theo possesses the mindset that many can benefit from. Theo taps into many innovative ways to leverage his money and create wealth. With Theo's investment properties, he produces safe space for his tenants. With his stock portfolio, he is able to produce generational wealth. By listing his car on a short-term rental website, he is able to provide reliable transportation for community members to drive to work. In addition, by selling old clothes and shoes online, Theo creates sustainable recycling measures and provides name brand apparel at affordable prices.

A producer creates income not only for themselves, but, for others in their community as well. Now, keep in mind, Theo makes $70,000 a year. He earns slightly less then Rico. However, he has a "producer mindset". Theo uses his income to buy rental properties, flip houses, and purchase stocks. Moreover, he then creates various streams of income by leveraging his mindset. Theo offers consultant services. And, he sells many items online as well. Theo truly makes his money work for him all while holding down a full-time job. Theo is creating a legacy. Soon his investments will pay more than his day job. Once Theo reaches this level of success, he will be able to quit his day job and work full-time for himself. Once Theo goes into business for himself and makes "Boss Moves", he can then produce jobs for his friends and family. Theo is on the path to becoming self-made, self-reliable, and self-sufficient.

To become a successful producer, you must first change your mindset.

A producer should be able to produce jobs, resources and services. Being a producer is a selfless position because you are constantly creating for others.

3. ASSET VS. LIABILITY

Liability = car note, mortgage debt, bank debt, rent, money owed, taxes, etc.

A liability is anything that will take money out of your pockets. Rico had a lot of liabilities listed in his monthly expenses. The goal is to have ZERO liabilities and MANY Assets. Zero liabilities mean not investing in a high-interest car that will have little to zero resale value. Zero liabilities mean not investing in high designer fashion with low resale value. Zero liabilities mean not purchasing an expensive watch that can tell the same time as your phone. Zero liabilities mean not purchasing thousand dollar shoes that are trendy this year and will be out of season next year. Zero liabilities mean not spending an enormous amount of money at the most popular lounge, bar, or club that will never hire you. Zero liabilities is an essential term that means you should only focus on purchasing items that will create income. You should only spend your money in your community and on items that you definitely need.

"He who owns the assets makes the rules."

Asset= cash, investment, equity, real estate, and stocks.

An asset is anything that will add money to your pockets. We should have zero liabilities and many assets. We have to channel our minds to focus on financial literacy. We have worked for money for far too long. The time is now to let money work for us.

Assets are a different kind of investment. What you reap is what you sow. What you put in is what you get out. So, to have appreciating assets, you must first learn how to invest. Investing is an art and a life long tool that will help you obtain generational wealth. Investing is a projected guess backed by time and money.

Investor mindset:

Franklin notices his neighborhood is changing. Old buildings are being knocked down and new buildings are springing up. This is an obvious sign of gentrification. It's important to combat gentrification by buying land and houses in your community. Purchasing these assets will help you gain ownership in your community and it will also produce jobs in your community as well. To really benefit from gentrification you must buy low and sell high. Shift your mindset to stop buying useless liabilities and instead start purchasing assets to truly live a life of freedom!

4. REAL ESTATE AND LAND

"Fortune befriends the bold."-Emily Dickinson

Ronald: Lives in a lovely high-rise apartment downtown.
Jeff: Owns 3 properties and 5 acres of land.

Ronald pays $2,500 a month to reside in his beautiful 1 bedroom, 1 bathroom, 550 square foot, hi-rise apartment downtown. In a year, Ron would have paid $30,000 to the property owner of the apartment complex. Ron decides to live in his apartment for three years. Rent increases by 3% every year.

Ron first year rent:	$30,000
Ron second year rent:	$30,900
Ron third year rent:	$31,800
Total:	$92,700

When Ronald vacates his lease after a three (3) year term. He would have paid his landlord $92,700.

Jeff notices new buildings being constructed in his neighborhood. But, unlike Ronald, Jeff has a producer mindset. So, Jeff wants to profit from the new construction erecting in his neighborhood. Jeff begins to buy cheap unattractive homes in his community. Jeff also takes an interest in the raw land as well. As a result, Jeff gives himself a few months to save money and build credit in order to fulfill his dream to buy up the block.

Jeff buys his first house:	$30,000
Jeff buys a second house:	$35,000
Jeff buys a third house:	$20,000
Jeff buys 5 acres of land:	$5,000
Total:	$90,000

Property ownership is key! Since Jeff built his credit score, he is now able to apply for a bank loan to fix all 3 of his properties. Once the necessary repairs are made to the properties, Jeff will then be able to flip the homes and earn serious income!

Jeff sells house 1 for	$60,000
Jeff sells house 2 for:	$78,000
Jeff sells house3 for:	$35,000
Jeff sells 5 acres for:	$17,500
Total:	$190,500

Jeff's income started at $90,000. However, with a Producer's mindset, Jeff was able to generate $100,500 in profits.

Now, Jeff has a gross income of $190,500.

Let's revisit Ron. As a renter, Ron used his income of $92,700 and made $0. Actually, Ron's lifestyle created more debt given his rent increases year-over-year.

If we understand how to effectively buy and sell real estate/land, we can build assets and gain wealth. Jeff decided to purchase stressed real estate in his community. Once he repaired the homes, he "flipped" them for greater profits, and he sold them. Jeff could have equally decided to rent the homes to families seeking to rent renovated properties. This option would have also generated income for Jeff as well. When acquiring assets, you can use many different strategies to generate positive cash flow.

5. INVESTMENT

"The rich will never allow me to eat with them and discuss their business ideas with me. But they will put their knowledge in a book."- Chukwuemeka Nwaopara

Before you invest your money into any area of interest, first do extensive research on the topic. It is imperative that you always research the pros, cons, laws, rules, business licensing processes, as well as the good, the bad, and the ugly.

Before you spend any money, it would benefit you to buy books and research the property that you are trying to acquire. Extensive research is key! It is always a best business practice to purchase books from the top performers in your market. Save yourself time by learning from the mistakes of professionals. Watch online videos to become more familiar with your subject matter to gain the most from your investment. Always remember to fight fear with action! You should not be afraid to invest. You should not be afraid to be a producer.

In the last chapter, Jeff was not afraid to invest $90,000. This allowed him to double his cash flow. However, to the contrary, Ron was fearful to invest. As a result, he lost $92,700. Therefore, you should always have a producer mindset.

You should use your mind to produce jobs, resources, assets, and investments.

6. CREDIT

Credit is something you must build. You must understand how credit works. It's equally important to understand how to leverage credit as well. Good credit can help you obtain better loan options. It will also give you better opportunities.

Ryan Credit Score = 800
Sam Credit Score = 534

Ryan and Sam are visiting a car dealership. They are interested in purchasing the same car at the same price. Both have budgeted the same amount of money to spend on the vehicle. They both work the same job and have identical salaries. The only difference is their credit score.

New car = $20,000
Ryan interest rate= 2.69%
Sam interest rate = 23.00%

Ryan monthly car note payment = $357/5 years
Sam monthly car note payment = $564 /5 years

Ryan ends up paying: $21,420.
Sam ends up paying: $33,840

In this example, you see the importance of having good credit. Since Sam's credit score was much lower than Ryan's credit score, he was given a higher interest rate to pay. As a result, Sam will pay $12,420 more than Ryan for the exact same car.

7. TAXES

"America's greatest expense is – TAXES"

The average American will spend approximately 33% of their wealth on paying taxes. We are taxed when we make money. We are taxed when we spend money. Crazy enough, we are sometimes taxed when we save money. It is so necessary to understand how to navigate taxes and tax write-offs. You must study the IRS tax laws and learn the many ways to write-off line items from your tax sheet to lower your "Taxable Income". Once you are able to successfully lower your taxable income, you will begin to pay lower taxes. Leveraging tax write-offs should be your ultimate goal. If you open a business, you will be able to enjoy multiple benefits of tax write-offs. This is the primary reason why I encourage everyone to start a business!

Owning a business will allow you to receive various tax write-offs. Some of them are 100% tax-deductible such as: advertising/promotion, business meals, business insurance, business interest, business car use, depreciation, education, home office, bank interest, legal fees, professional fees, moving expenses, rent expense, salaries, telephone/internet expense, travel expense, and personal expense. I would highly encourage you to take advantage of these tax write-offs.

Otherwise, you will continue to give IRS your hard-earned money year-over-year.

8. FAMILY BUSINESS

A family business is an entity in which all members should have the same underlying goal, which is to create generational wealth. Financial literacy is key in a family business model. Each member must have a producer mindset. Each family business should only purchase assets and zero liabilities. Moreover, each person in the family business should be disciplined and focused on the goal in order to succeed. All eyes must always remain on the prize.

The goal is to have a self-sufficient family. You should build your family business to survive the competition, leverage resources, create jobs, and master the power of spending. Financial literacy is very important and will shape your mindset for the better. You must work with your family to create generational wealth. You must produce a service and leverage the strengths of your family.

A family business will build a stronger bond in your family. All family members must be on the same page. The goal must be long term and not short term. If you have a producer mindset, greed should not wind its way into the equation. With a long-term focal point, you must understand that the goal is to create generational wealth and not to compete with one another.

9. FINANCIAL FREEDOM

Here is a topic that is not discussed enough in our community LIFE INSURANCE! Please make sure everyone in your family has a proper life insurance policy to cover essential needs at the time of death. Generational wealth is created by a thought and a mindset. We must first think about generational wealth. Then we must create it!

Generation after generation, we find ourselves struggling trying to work for someone else. This places us in a starting position at the bottom instead of at the top. A lot of issues occur by purchasing too many liabilities. We must shape our mindset to build something for our kids' kids. Keep in mind, the places where you spend your hard-earned money is already building wealth for their generation. And, you are helping them to fund their dreams. This ends today! To create generational wealth, you must work to be self-sufficient. You must link arms with your family and people in your community to create this shift!

We must invest as a family, think like producers, leverage assets as a family, and create businesses together to create sustainable financial ecosystems. We must work together to accomplish goals as one. This is how we go "From the Hood to Owning Hollywood".

ABOUT THE AUTHOR

Chukwuemeka Nwaopara is a driven and successful real estate investor, professional consultant, and entrepreneur. He has a huge passion for entrepreneurship and loves sharing financial literacy tips with young adults.

Mr. Nwaopara leads a dynamic book club called Wise Kings where members discuss financial literacy, mental health, generational wealth, family structure, and social justice. When time permits, Chukwuemeka loves to swim, cycle, and hike.

Chukwuemeka currently resides in Atlanta, Georgia where he is working on his next book.

You may stay connected with Chukwuemeka by visiting his website at: www.MajesticCyberEnterprises.com

To book Chukwuemeka for speaking engagements, please send an email to: MajesticCyberEnterprises@gmail.com.

Thank you, for purchasing my book. I hope you learned some good tips about financial literacy. Please leave a review. I read every review personally. Thanks so much for your support!